Pop-Up Book of Death

POP-UP BOOK OF DEATH

Chad Helder

A Rebel Satori Imprint
Bar Harbor, Maine

REBEL SATORI PRESS
P.O. Box 363
Hulls Cove, ME 04644
www.rebelsatori.com

Acknowledgments:
"Blizzard" and "Public Service Announcement" appeared in
    Hand.Tooth.Nail.
"The Day We Met" and "Persona" appeared in Crosscurrents.
"Spam Campaign," "Gorgeous Metamorphosis," "I'm Craig
    the Plumber's Incompetent Helper," "My Paper Boy is
    a Vampire," "Ghost," and "The Undertow" appeared in
    Pixartisan.

Book design by Sven Davisson

Library of Congress Cataloging-in-Publication Data

Helder, Chad, 1973-
  The pop-up book of death / Chad Helder.
      p. cm.
  ISBN 978-1-60864-026-3 (pbk.)
  I. Title.
  PS3608.E3855P66 2010
  811'.6--dc22
                                    2010043507

Dedication:
For Tshombé

Special thanks:

to Jim Doyle for introducing me to writing poetry and being a wonderful poetry mentor, to Bruce Beasley for being an excellent and subversive poetry teacher, to Rita Kiefer for introducing me to the poetry of Ai (my favorite poet and first poetry love), to Sean for lots of great feedback again, to Bernard Dewley for inspiration and for publishing my poems, to Marcus Slease for reading some of these poems in graduate school, to Jim for being an enthusiastic reader of my poems and for lots of encouragement, to my friends at Village Books, to Janie for starring in my Postmodern Literature Camp dream, to my friend Steph who read my first poems and profoundly encouraged me, to Sven Davisson for taking on this book, to Steve Berman for telling me about Queer Mojo in the first place, to my super-supportive family, and to Robin for letting me share the story.

CONTENTS

THE RIVER

A group of mourners,
standing on the riverbank,
rise from the page like
flowers in time lapse photography.
Even if the page is opened quickly,
the paper figures emote bereavement.

A clever optical illusion:
the lines of the river trick the eye into seeing
relentless current, which
continues to flow in a blink
like the echo of a flash bulb.

Pull the tab:
A pursuit of crocodile and corpse ensues to the right.
The paper body and reptilian scavenger ride on a track,
bobbing up and down through a cut in the page.
At the end of the track, a crocodile jumps from the left,
nipping the thumb of the reader with a sharp cardboard edge.

A fun activity:
The Crocodile Death Roll Game for the bathtub.

ORIGINS OF BURIAL

A Neanderthal corpse rises up from the page
(two edges of paper rub together to simulate a deathcough).

Pull the tab:
The corpse curls into the fetal position.
If the page is left open overnight,
moonlight will awaken the microscopic organisms
placed on this page at the factory.
In the morning, your child will discover the miracle of
    decomposition
(god's erasure)
and the mystery implement of the Neanderthal's death
(a bear's tooth? an arrow head?)
which is easily crafted into a necklace.
Lift the flaps to discover
more artifacts to accompany loved ones to the next world.

A fun activity:
Bury a friend in the fetal position.

EGYPTIAN HEAD

The bandages slide away like worms to reveal the grinning head.

Pull the nose tab:
Learn the Egyptian secret of unraveling the brain with a hook
    through the nostril.

Learn the effects of moisture on corpses and the
(amazing)
quick rot of the floater.

A Fun Activity:
Monkey traps and the secret to shrunken heads.

Wear your heads like a necklace.

THE VOID

Don't allow children under the age of ten to stare at this page unsupervised.

WAGES OF SIN

A scaffold rises from the page,
complete with dangling criminal on a string
and a mobile of circling vultures.

Blow:
and the vultures close in.

Pull the tab:
The trap door releases.
The prisoner's eyeballs and tongue pop out
(Warning: Choking Hazard for children under the age of three).
The bloodthirsty mob rises from the page
and shakes fists at the hapless soul.

Learn about loss of bladder control in the chair
and gross jobs for Death Row janitors.

MARTYRDOM

The pyre rises from the page,
complete with kindling (matches not included).
A set of cut-out cardboard martyrs can be found
in the back of the book.
The platform is treated with the latest fire retardant material,
so your child can reuse the platform again and again
for martyr-burning fun
(parental supervision recommended;
keep away from curtains).

DEATH AND YOU

The mirror:
Finger face paints in shades of gray
line the side of the page.
Affix a spot of fungus to your face.
Tear the perforations to remove the paper glasses that
turn your eyes to holes.
Like a funhouse mirror,
the reader's face distorts into pain and
regret.

Pull the tab:
Worms wriggle out the reflection.

DOG BOY

As a dog boy,
I played fort in my closet
where a weird menagerie of monkey puppets
and puppy centerfolds gazed down upon me.

I wore the brown socks of the preacher's son,
and pulled on an accepted identity
like a tight football helmet.

But pretty soon
beastly desire betrayed
my award winning disguise
while puberty spun dark hairs down my legs.

As my voice deepened, so did the desire,
but I only knew
the eager wet lapping of the dog boy,
never the gulping satisfaction of the Wolf Man.

As a dog boy,
I ventured outside the fortress of my closet
only to find more passages,
and my closet transmogrified into a labyrinth.
Every time I looked behind,
I found the sharp raccoon tracks of my miseries
in pursuit.

Then I found the beautiful curves of your footprints
in the luscious muddy ground.
I followed your tracks with my dog boy steps.

You offered your hand,
and our union was like
the profound grip of the trapeze artist.

You led me over the boundaries of the labyrinth
to the canopy-path above:
the joyous leaping of the parachute squirrel.
I held on to you like a Tarsier,
and you showed me a gorgeous metamorphosis
like Beauty's kiss
from dog boy to Wolf Man.

We howl.
Luxurious coats beneath the full moon.

Now we share
delectable and nourishing meat;
forget forever
the hard nuggets rattling
in the porcelain bowl
of the dog boy.

BOY AND HIS DOG

I place my face inside her skull-mask
as I peer through the blur-hair;
the blizzard of her bangs
descends over my eyes
in white-out erasure.

I crawl into the dog,
a costume,
a silky white cocoon.

My foamy tongue dangles past my chin,
and I am helpless to tuck it back inside my lips.
The passages inside my nose branch and turn,
multiplying into the labyrinth
of the dog's odor-understanding.

I feel the white hair blear the clarity of my eyes,
and I transmogrify into the dog again
just like the old movie with Tommy Kirk.

I place the white dog costume
between myself and the camera
in this black-and-white family comedy.
I place the white dog's mammalian warmth
between myself and the world.
Her image, her symbol, the idea of the white dog
filters my secret.

Her hair turns as black as a shadow,
as black as a pubic hair
with what the white dog filters.

The white dog costume
bleaches my fear of the dark.
I clutch her like a flotation device
as the shadow flash floods the neighborhood.
She buoys me up from the drowning,
buoys me up like a coffin
in which you will find me.

GHOST

The ghost of the dog might
electrify the context
like the sharp barking in my brain,
leave the sign of her paw on strange mud
in the text of this dream landscape.

The dog, now transmuted into symbol,
a phantom in the landscape
where we stand at the edge of the bay together.
She barks in excitement like applause
and wags the tail docked off at birth.
I see a remnant stump moving beneath her coat,
the tail entirely absent,
except for a steadfast dog-mind notion
of its existence.
Now all the dog is absent,
and the notion romps in my brain.
The moisture of her nose and the sniffing at my ear
tickle like the missing foot
at the bottom of the amputated leg, only real
when our minds build phantoms with pieces.
She barks in excitement at the whales
and the clapping of their tails,
harbingers from the ocean in my skull,
the ultimate symbols of the subliminal
where the messages emerge:
terrible water spouts on the horizon,

the rising of the Great White for the final severance,
and the recurring image of the ambiguous Killer Whale
to swallow me in some dreams
and to free me from the drowning plunge in others.

But today, the tails and spouts react in chorus,
as if the whale ear knows the bell of her bark.
She evokes these signs of good fortune
from the water void beneath visibility.
Is every hair accounted for in this phantom incarnation?
When the dog joined the ground,
she evaporated into the phantom symbol, the dream sign,
an embodiment of lost time.
Her collar and leash, hanging on my bedroom door
would rattle at the intruder's entrance.
I run my hand through the unknowable proliferation of her
        mantle.
I awake from the dream with a white hair in my mouth.

BIRTHDAY CAKE

The intruder enters the front door
during the wine and cheese party.
The guests turn to me to do something
before someone gets killed.
The hostess of the party leads me to her bedroom
where she keeps her bullet drawer.

Right above the sock drawer,
the bullet drawer contains rows of bullets,
all dressed in colorful knit outfits
like finger puppets.
I undress six of the bullets and load my gun.

I return to the party to kill the intruder;
I discover the intruder has transformed
into my boyhood dog,
but she is old and sick.
The execution has become a mercy killing
to put the dog out of her misery.

She doesn't know what's happening
as I put the gun to the back of her head.
I pull the trigger several times,
but the gun does not fire.
It only makes flat-sounding thuds.
I open the gun to discover
the chamber is clogged with birthday cake.

MY DOG EARNS HER PH.D.

My dog Panda comes back from the grave
to earn her Ph.D. in Literature.

I ask Panda how many dogs have their doctorate.
She makes a "U" shaped sign with her tongue,
which I interpret to mean two,
and she barks to indicate this is correct.
Wow
only the third dog to ever earn a doctoral degree.

I feel guilty
because I always treated her like a dog,
just played fetch with a squeaky rubber boot.
I never attempted to foster any interest in literature,
unaware of her scholarly aptitude.

I ask Panda about her doctoral thesis.
She writes it on my forehead with a wet tongue.
This is how dogs communicate in academia.

TRAILER PARK

In the end I am a trailer park whore.
The Lord God formed a covenant
with the mice beneath the floor.

I once tried to put down the suffering dog,
but its anguish grows.
My newspaper is wet every day.

I once knew the thrill
of another boy's stubble
and tracing the vein down his arm.
Now I know too much about plumbing
and obstructions.

GUTTER BOY

I remember
my locker partner's black curly hair,
elf-face of adolescence,
dynamic pimples on his nose.

I teased him;
I called him Gutter Boy.

He got into trouble in algebra for saying dildo.
The teacher told him to stop,
but he repeated the word and
refused to believe it meant more than nonsense.

The teacher refused to define it,
which he took as evidence.

I knew what dildo meant.
I explained it to him in the hall by our locker.
I called him Gutter Boy after that.

The doctors amputated his right leg for cancer.

He wore a prosthetic leg with a diaphragm mechanism,
walked with a limp,
played with the air bladder in the mechanism:
loud farting noises.
He showed off the mechanism by

kicking the locker in the hallway:
loud tympanic crashes.

He joked
he could kick an imaginary attacker in the crotch.
He astounded onlookers by
sticking a pencil in the knee,
kicking the leg out, and
shattering the pencil into fragments
like a bone after a fall from a cliff.

I carried the teasing too far one day;
I said his penis was so gigantic that
the doctors had to chop off the leg just to
fill up the fake leg
with his whale-sized dick.
He wouldn't speak to me after algebra that day.
No more Gutter Boy jokes.

They performed a terrible operation;
they sawed through his sternum,
opened his chest,
extracted cancerous lung pieces.

I noticed
a tip of scar tissue peeking up from his shirt collar
like a penis tip from underwear.

I imagined peeking underneath his shirt
to gaze at the chest scar diagram
like forbidden black magic drawings.

Then in the dream,
on the date at Lover's Lane,
Gutter Boy gazed into my eyes:
the intensity and confusion
and the kissing,
a confusion of bumping tongues like
fish in a net;
I pulled back from the kiss
to see his eyes,
discovering how
only in a dream
can the long snout,
jagged formations of teeth,
and hot pasty tongue of my dog
feel like the mouth of a boy.

THE OWL BY THE CHURCH

Beneath the great tree by the church,
the sheepdog leads the boy
under the Satan in the owl's eye,
past a molded omen of rodent skulls and hair
that fell from the bough
where a wicked sculptor waits
in his house of owl innards,
waits
to turn pink mice into prey,
into clay,
and the boy lifts the flap of the sheepdog's ear,
whispers to the Jesus in the pink canyon underneath,
to a sculptor of secret dog ears and pink mice
that later grow corrupt and covered in hair.

A stranger steps from behind the wide trunk,
an emergence from shadow,
to flash the boy a mouse
he holds in his hand.

INSTEAD

I wanted to be your best friend in the fifth grade,
your best friend and more.

We walked home from school together one day.
I admired your glasses
with the tiny Superman crests at the joints,
so I told my parents I needed glasses too,
but my vision turned out to be too perfect
for glasses like yours.
I admired your red hair
and pale cheeks,
not always flushed with blood like mine.

At the sleepover,
I tripped over the rope
and ripped the tent in your back yard,
but your dad didn't even get mad.
The lightning flashed
and possessed your hand-held computer game,
so we went inside and watched 2001 with your dad,
all three of us completely bored until
the computer goes mad and murders the astronauts.

The bully-ogre named Dickie
punched your face on the playground
and broke your glasses
and stepped on your new baseball cap.

I dreamed of championing your revenge.
On Halloween we tiptoed past his house,
(no lights on for trick-or-treaters),
and I was sure he would smell intruders
and chase us down the street.

And I loved you like only a ten-year-old boy
can love his best friend.

But something mysterious
from beneath
began to gain
definition and momentum,
as threatening as
a whale breach, so I pushed it down,
and it sounded into the depth again,
remaining undefined:
it emanated from you,
entangled everything around you,
your speech and your skin
and coiled in your bedroom where
I stood and thought:
so this is where he slips beneath the covers,
and this is the nightstand
where he sets down his glasses until morning.

And you wanted to be my best friend too,
but the threat of exposure grew inside me—
I already knew then
there was something wrong with me.

And then my dad gave me the Old English Sheepdog puppy;
the dog enabled me to deflect the desire,

and I built
a fortress,
and I ignored you
to play fetch,
and I chose my dog over you because
a dog is much safer than a boy
for someone like me.

Of course you found another best friend.

You took him rock climbing with your dad
in the river-carved canyon where
your new best friend slipped on the rocks,
and when your dad went to save him,
your dad fell all the way down
to his death,
and your new best friend regained his footing.

I walked my dog past your house.
People gathered after the funeral
in your front yard.
You approached me on the sidewalk,
told me the story
about your dad's fall,
and I didn't believe you.

You asked, why do you think all those people are in my yard?
I looked at the people—all of them dressed in black.

I walked my dog past your house again.
I saw you crying on your uncle's shoulder
beneath the shade tree.
I wanted to say I'm sorry for not believing you,

but your uncle waved me away.

It was my first job in the restaurant kitchen;
I washed dishes there with the boy who slipped.
One night he stopped in the middle of spraying silverware
to say it was the worst moment of his life
when the Sheriff told him your dad was dead.

That night in your dorm room years later
when we were both freshman at the university:

when I took rum shuts until I blacked out,
and you told me
you wanted to be best friends
in the fifth grade too,
but all I wanted to do was play with my dog;

when we secretly danced to Morrissey,
and I wanted to kiss you as we
collapsed drunk on the floor,
but I knew you didn't like boys like I did;

when I cried in front of your suite mates
as I veered closer to blackout,
cried about your father's horrible fall,
cried about my own father's departure
to distant volcanic islands;

when I knew it couldn't happen like I wanted,

and I cried because I was a stupid boy
who chose my dog in the fifth grade,
and maybe I wouldn't have slipped

on the rocks that day in the canyon
if I had been there,
if I had been your best friend
instead.

SUNDAY IN BROWN SOCKS

Tissue-thin Bible pages crackle in the background of the radio
    show.
The narrator's voice escapes from the underworld through the
    airwaves.
Any Christian can tune in.
My brain sprouts supernatural transmitters,
and He hears me when I think His name.
I know His operatives listen
because the Ouija Board knows my birthday.

Satan crashed our Malibu by remote control,
and when I cracked my forehead on the dashboard,
His voice electrified me through the speaker in the door.

Sometimes, on Sunday mornings,
I wake with my head in a concrete block
that tastes chalky,
but I can pace it away in brown socks and a tie.
Before service, I stand in the sanctuary
where the orange pews buzz like madness.
Staring one-eyed through red stained glass,
I know how Satan sees the churchyard.

The council implanted a secret microphone in the minister's
    throat.
He took it like a pill,
and the device clutched his vocal chords

with hundreds of microscopic prongs.
Now his voice thunders in the sanctuary,
drowning out the tiny voices during hymns.
But during prayer, when the congregation seals their eyes,
a force disrupts the transmission.
The device malfunctions,
and I see his lips move to different words
while slivers of smoke leak out a nostril.

Downstairs, after service,
the children line up for watery punch.
Jim Jones has returned from hibernation.
I put teeth marks in my Styrofoam cup,
and underneath my Kool Aid mustache
hides a forked tongue
stained the color of cherry.

BLIZZARD

I restrained the secret like a cough,
afraid my family might catch confusion,
tucked it inside my pillowcase
where it knocked on my head for attention,
hid it beneath layers
like hypothermia prevention,
and kept it in my pocket,
a revolver
I didn't know where to point.

Then the secret passed its puberty,
and a bass voice shook
the flying buttresses of my brain.

I kissed you on the Ping-Pong table,
the first peculiar thrill
of another boy's stubble
and touched the blue vein
in the crook in your arm.

But I wrote "attracted" and "attached"
on the note I slipped in your locker.
You replied "neither,"
and I meant "attached" like a twin
the doctors can't separate.

I treated first love like hopeless CPR.

And my mind fell
like a blizzard
that entombed the secret over
again.

LOVE POEM

I catch your hand in the blind twirling
of the trapeze masterpiece,
the slippery pitfall dance
of the acrobats;
your love rescues me from
drowning
in the feeding frenzy of applause
beneath.

The magic of your love awakens hopeless hibernations;
your love transforms the coma to ballet,
tracheotomy rattle to the gorgeous moaning of bassoons.

SPAM CAMPAIGN

Suddenly
mothers everywhere dropped their babies
flower stalks snapped in half
and
cocker spaniels knocked radios into bathtubs
just because
you received another rejection letter

you know your sorrow has twin engines
and you learned the wrong lesson from the flight attendants
always looking for
emergency exit rows
inflatable seat cushions
and the miraculous falling oxygen bag
with the cup like tin-can-telephone
which happens to be
the official language of your country
(you funneled my spam campaigns
and my heart
into the deleted items folder)

and it's another crisis in the maximum security prison
of your mind
and your life is like a sperm in a freezer bag

I just wish you would stop being such an
abandoned theme park

such an emotional clear cut
such an ever-descending helicopter pod

so please come in out of the rain
I'll never warm you in the microwave
we'll start over again
we'll max out credit cards
we'll raise retarded children
and travel hand in hand to
basically inactive volcanic islands

we'll snuggle together like two names forever
in the upper-left-hand
corner of the checkbook

NEANDERTHAL LOVE

tender Neanderthal loving
in a Paleolithic fantasy of
undraping bearskins

you tend the campfire
in the mouth of the cave to deter
ravenous bears
bloodthirsty wolf packs
tool-wielding homo sapiens and
the violation
of the present now
where only your extinction
walks

in my high school anthropology class
I first learned your name
as Mrs. Hartman demonstrated
the evolution of upright walking and
showed overhead projections
of the heavy brow ridge
that housed your heavenly eyes

even the best forensic skull sculptors
can't capture
the precocious magic
of your smile

I wander past
the glass walls of
museum dioramas
your wax-figure likeness
posed in the context of
straight anthropologist fictions:
caveman squalor
all nuclear families
while ominous sabertooth horrors
lurk above
in frozen taxidermy

I know
some Neanderthal men
loved men
because I tasted your sweet kisses
beneath a primordial moon
after you skinned the bear for me and
made a necklace of claws
by the fireside

you showed me the secret:
the Darwinian advantage
of gay love
which they omitted on purpose
from my human evolution textbook

when I first held
the cast of your skull
my heart ached to see
the empty orbital sockets and
I traced the brow ridge with my fingertip

kissed the absent lips
as if you were my lost Yorrick

for the first time I forgot
about Eve
when you and I
joined together
in the dewy grasses of Eden
like two branches
made inextricable

today
I still feel your echo
in my ancestry
as I tread alone:
my tender feet
matching your fossilized footprints
leading me beyond
the Garden of Expulsion

PERSONA

Cryptic marginalia litters the manuscript
on the desk in front of the persona:
geometric designs with lumpings of triangles.
In some places, the marginal scribbles appear to
obliterate the actual text.
The strings of triangles often
suggest maelstroms of teeth.
The bundles of circles in the hieroglyphic marginalia
hint at sacs of eggs or the prolific horror
of the ovipositor.
Grids of varying intricacy
suggest not only screens that prevent exit,
but the pins and the restricting structures of traction.
The lines:
sinews and strings of connective tissue.
The closer the proliferation of circles,
the more a fly-eyed sense of surveillance
pervades the scene.
Certain words appear to have texture.
The word "placid" might appear in the text,
but we know the reason for this:
the reader can strike a match on it
(a textual gimmick for smokers in the reading audience,
but secretly for the arson,
for the inmates to ignite the bed sheets).
Like a reef,
certain lines will founder the tip of a pencil,

sink holes lurk in the margins.
Trapdoor spiders will strike from beneath the word
"multivalence"
to inject poison in a fingertip
(The eggs hatch in the spine).
And landmines will blow the digits off anyone touching
the text with an orange highlighter pen.
The persona recites this poem with hand gestures
resembling
to flatten clay or to set a bird free.

FIELD NOTES ON NEWSSTAND WILDLIFE

On the top row, in the far corner
behind sweaty sports weeklies
and crafty homemaking seasonals
that reek of potpourri,
the peculiar bird constructs its nest.
Running errands to the outside,
the bird returns from scavenging
with a beakful of objects to add to the pile:

Frilly panties discovered in the glove box
of a humid Ford Mustang.
A shard of mirror chipped off a bedroom ceiling.
Pointed wires and resonating springs
from a deluxe dildo.
A dripping retina pecked out of a voyeur
who slept near open windows.
A bus ticket to Los Angeles
found in a cheerleader's pocket.
A flailing anal hamster.
A photographer's index finger
that wouldn't stay on the camera.
A discarded engagement ring.

These items collected,
the bird secretes a pulpy fluid
to paste the nest together.

Confined to the top shelf during this process,
the bird sacrifices food,
but men in closed raincoats
offer supportive worms.

When the nest is finished,
the bird perches erect,
inflating an air sac
like rubber-raft titties
to attract mates.
Similar to bees on flowers,
the customers unknowingly fertilize
with trembling paranoid fingers.

FEAR OF SPIDERS

At last I quit killing spiders,
despite the shudder squeal of
finding a hairy fellow
who shares the doorjamb.

The dread of the window well
where the Black Widow reigns:
I tried to kill her with a pole;
I tried to kill her with a shovel,
only to find her scrambling up the handle
toward the tender hand
of the invader.

The plumber told me:
the nurses cut him out of his jeans at the ER.
The Black Widow bit his leg
while he plumbed in her subterranean crevice.

And my brother's nightmare
about spiders in wax from the hotdog vendor
at the ballpark.

The horror of the bulbous abdomen
and spike-legs like Vlad the Impaler's pikes:
the witch's blood hourglass on your belly,
great femme fatale of the arachnid world.

As a child I smashed many spiders
to see the color of their blood,
and in the nightmare,
the great Spider God
dropped each resurrected victim
into the coffin
of my premature burial.

The Daddy Longlegs my only spider friend.

Much maligned and stereotyped,
the spider is not the preying Nosferatu
of apocalyptic mutants in the age of Cold War despair,
but the patient slurper of bountiful juice pouches
dropped from the sky
by generous gods
on artisan tapestries.

Now I never kill a spider
as a rule—
when I clean out the shadows
of my fear,
I always find them spinning silken altars
to offer up their sacrifices
to the landlord: me,
and I find them
waiting
like happy little crossing guards on lawn chairs,
only too happy to assist a juicy grasshopper
to the other side.

FUNERAL

I depicted the funeral of my grandfather
in my elementary school story.

The shining, uniform white squares
of my grandfather's false teeth.

His raspy laugh
and white beard.

I sat with him on the couch
as he fixed the fire alarm;
he held it in his hand and
blew cigarette smoke inside
to make it scream.

The spectacular array of colorful medications
for his heart condition.

The pale statue-wax look of his inert hands
in the casket.

I viewed the body.

Some great-uncle said
I should touch Grandpa's hands,
touch the dead hands

as cold as the earth,

but the earth is fire too:
the core erupts through volcanoes.

I touched his hands;
they felt like bread.

IN THE SUMMER OF THE FLYING GRASSHOPPERS

Once, after the third grade
I slept over at Richard's house
when he showed me
his failed science project, asked me
to guess. I guessed volcanic debris
and petrified wood and fossilized scat,
but it was only a normal hot dog twisted
in the intensity of the oven. Richard's mother
left his ears exposed, and I
envied his haircut. On the swing set we
talked about the movie with the surprising
array of boobs. Richard laughed through his nose,
and a glob of milky-white snot landed on his upper lip, but
he didn't try to hide it.
He smiled like an elf
and made a web of it between his fingers.
I gagged and puked into his mother's strawberries.
He apologized for the disgust,
but I puked out of surprise.

The next morning he chewed his toenails
in front of the television, and I watched,
astonished
at the audacity and flexibility,
an embarrassing contortion of skinny legs
I could never try.

His mother set off the fire alarm
with burning bacon and woke up
the father who trotted downstairs in amused concern,
not a gorilla rampage at the disruption.

It was that summer of the flying grasshoppers,
and Richard meant
to torture one.
It escaped up into an unreachable corner of the garage
near the ceiling, but in a miracle shot,
Richard nailed it with a warm handful of putty.

We first exploded
in laughter, then watched for juice to leak from beneath
the flattened wad, but none came—the putty sealed it tight,
smashed the grasshopper like a microscope slide,
and I imagined peeling back the putty to reveal
a kaleidoscope impression of grasshopper parts,
an exquisite symmetry
entombed above my reach.

FISH TANK WOLFMAN

In the bookstore basement
the owner keeps a fish tank

I discover the action-figure-sized wolfman
pacing back and forth
on the glass bottom

Knowing the little wolfman can't breathe
down there
I flip open the lid to the fish tank

The Sasquatch-sized wolfman
climbs out of the tank
his brown hair streaming water
all over the floor of the bookstore basement

Towering above me
the gigantic wolfman thanks me
for releasing him from the spell
and he abandons me with all the puddles

and I know the owner will fire me for sure
when he sees the puddles
and finds out it was me
who released his secret wolfman

POSTMODERNIST CAMP

At Postmodernist Literature Camp,
someone broke into my cabin and
vivisected my bunk bed like a birthday cake.

Doug disappeared into the forest
to find illumination.

We searched and couldn't find him,
so we returned to studying Literature.

When Doug finally emerged from the forest,
he had a terrible case of stigmata.

Fortunately, Janie had seen this before.

She removed a tube of stigmata ointment from her purse.

Janie has her Ph.D. in Literature.

BAT DREAM

At the supermarket
a new display of bats on sale

the small size rips open with a tear strip
like the resealable bags of shredded cheese
a little plastic ripcord
and inside a honeycomb of bat packaging

the bats fly out
the speed of hummingbird wings
like pouring out the cremated on wind
and the air zips with bat wings

the medium size
packaged with egg carton
and frozen for freshness
a three-pack of bats
each a winged little fetus

and the large size bat
hangs from a hooked claw
like an obscene hairless chew toy

and I'm relieved because
I get one at last
before they sell out
and I tuck the naked urchin
under my arm

48

to be resurrected at home
with warm water

CHIROPTERA

If I could be you
Chiroptera
bat god
for the crunch-juice of exoskeleton
in a mouth of needle-teeth

for the exquisite beauty
sound-sight texture of trees

all my screams would reflect back vision
instead of spilling away

the queer inverse world of the bat in the shadows
where now I collide with tree trunks
I might instead see
the ballet of moth wings with
the flashback music of your voice-vision

the membrane of my hand-wing would brush
past the lips of my sleeping lover
like a flower petal

as a boy I had a daydream about a bat as a pet
a gothic flying fox
I kept hanging in my closet like an umbrella

now I would open you
release you like a kite

if only the world of the bats allowed me inside
to join the secret legion of underground nuzzling

my zoo cards arrived in the mail
and I collected the images of your faces
weird people of the Chiroptera microbats
tender leaf-noses as delicate as genitals
the open sails of your ears to capture
vision like wind

if I could be a bat-shapeshifter
oh lord Chiroptera
allow me beneath
to shuffle inside the dance-floor ceiling
colony of bat lovers

all amassing
I invoke you all
Chiroptera and the taxonomy of your children
tonight
ready to awaken and spring
from the roof of my mouth-cave
like names

MY PAPER BOY IS A VAMPIRE

He delivers excellent service:
no more late morning sopping wads of newsprint
and pulp
in the bank of front porch snow.
Bit by some infectious other,
my tardy and dawdling paper boy passed away,
his blood and boyhood sucked out.

They buried him in a suit and a tie,
but the plucky vampire boy resurrected himself
and returned to his route,
barefoot through the snow,
delivering the papers in their polythene body bags.
The grave taught that boy the meaning
of good customer service.

Now he delivers the paper before my alarm clock crows
and the sunrise turns him to crisp bacon,
smiling with his beard of dried blood
like chocolate milk.

He comes to collect in the darkness
after the dinner hour.
I invite him inside
and awaken hours later
to find another twisty straw missing from the box,
and my shaving cut

trickling down my collar again.

My paper boy found a special talent
for drawing out the blood
from behind the words of the daily newspaper,
like an ape wringing moisture from a jungle leaf,
but he never learned the trick of cauterization,
and the words continue to weep blood like fresh stitches
as I read at my breakfast table,
and I find myself lapping up the dribbles
like a bat at a camper's toe,
like a loyal and satisfied customer.

THE VAMPIRE EXPERT

and the English Major's heart is still beneath the floorboards
in the English Professor's living room
pounding pounding

once a long time ago
a closeted English Major (that was me)
signed up for an independent study
to write horror stories
for the English Professor

you see the English Professor was a Vampire Expert
and a member of occult societies
and a practitioner of strange exorcisms

he professed his theory that the vampire archetype
originates from the unconscious anxiety
of the baby feeding off blood in the womb
and the repression of sucking on mother's breast
all transmogrified into bloodsucking shadow figures

and the Vampire Expert was
my ultimate horror mentor

and the Vampire Expert wore a black cape
and a slouch hat
and walked with a wolf's-head cane

he suggested we conduct
my independent study in his living room

he gave me a brandy snifter
and told me the best way to write good
vampire sex scenes
is to use personal experience
and he asked if my experience was with girls
or with boys
(he could see The Closet around me like a pall)
and he kept fishing for confidences
but I kept silent

and I noticed his elderly poodle had an erection

he was the ultimate horror mentor
and he taught me about
the archetypes of werewolf duality
and the thing-without-a-name of
Cold War anxieties
as we sipped our brandy
and he assigned me King's Danse Macabre to read
and I turned in my vampire homework

I wrote about the
coming-of-age vampire
who lost his belly button and
regained his foreskin
because he had been
reborn by the womb of the night
and now suckled at the mammary of darkness

and the Vampire Expert loved that detail

about the foreskin

and out of nowhere
the Vampire Expert told me I would
look good in a speedo

and the Vampire Expert told me he understood
the Power of the Shadow
and I believed him
but didn't want to know what he meant
scared to know what he meant

and the Vampire Expert felt pity for people
who really believed in vampires
and I agreed

he hated homonym errors and even gave Fs on papers
because of them so
I proofread very carefully

and the Vampire Expert hated Coppola's Dracula
because bloodsuckers aren't romantic
and he thought Tom Cruise was just OK as Lestat
because it should've been Rutger Hauer like Rice wanted
and I agreed

at the end of the semester I turned in my vampire story

and now I am just like him
obsessed with vampires
teaching Dracula every semester
looking at boys in speedos
composing theories about

archetypal patterns in the horror genre

and what did you mean about
the Power of the Shadow anyway
and maybe it would have been
OK to let you get into my pants
like you got into my brain

and maybe both of us have tell-tale hearts
still beating
beneath the floorboards
where an independent study
was conducted once
a long time ago

DREAMING THE KILLER

On the San Juan Islands day cruise,
I ate my overcooked salmon dinner
as the pod passed beneath us.
The woman across from me confessed
her interspecies identity disorder and
how she secretly was (in fact) a Spirit Orca herself;
she could feel the spectral blow hole on her back and
hear the call of the pod
with her mind's ear.

So later in the twilight return,
I told her about my Killer Whale nightmares
as a spy-hopper transient spotted our trespassing.

The evil Shamu head-muncher:
They put a swimming pool
in a Roman coliseum.
The gasping crowd watches the whales
jump through rings of fire,
the trainers all rodeo clowns in wetsuits.

For the final trick,
volunteers from the audience
march up a flight of stairs to the scaffold
where lucky tourists receive
a kiss from the deep,
except this time,

as the little boy
leans over the railing ,
the Killer Whale rises up and plucks
off his head like a cherry from its stem.

The coliseum rumbles in panic;
pillars fall and the rubble
buries tourists alive.

All of this inspired by the television documentary
about the transient mammal-eater
who steals baby seals off the beach.

In another dream,
I hold on to the Killer Whale's dorsal fin
as we rise from the depth
in a vision subconsciously misappropriated
from a sacred Native American tradition.

I find the dead whale in the
post-apocalyptic Sea World pool and
do a double take—
the pool now crowded with floating Indian corpses
of an All-American genocide.

I heard once that only half the Killer Whale's brain
sleeps at one time;
I devote both halves to them
during my somnambulant underwater
wanderings,
and half my mind
goes with them when I'm awake
and scrapes the bottom at Rubbing Beach.

They hit my clammy brain back and forth between their tails
like a dead baby seal as
the whale-watching motorboat traffic
paparazzis them to death
with rapid fire snapshot click flash.

Their tails splash my daydream brain
that earnestly tries to focus on traffic signals,
and sonar waves wash me like alarm clock calls
in reverse as
I submerge into my underwater pod-dream
where I find I hold my breath just fine
while nursing on an underwater nipple.

IN THE AFTERMATH OF YOUR SMILE

Sometimes poetry is like dentistry.
This time, however, I hold the metal spike,
and you, dear audience,
wait patiently in the chair,
wait patiently for the road construction
known as dentistry,
known as poetry.

My purpose here is not dental hygiene, I'm afraid,
but extraction,
to remove the white tiles from the hull of your smiles,
to arrive at the pronged root,
to arrive at the metaphor that all Dream Dictionaries
label:
the epicenter of the mystery.

It's official. I broke up with my dentist,
even though I still owe him three hundred dollars.

In the dream I accidentally pulled out my
tooth like
popping off a childproof Tylenol cap.
Underneath, a red sea anemone waited,
angry, pulsating with blood,
electrified like a nerve,
a dream-world harbinger of a crown-gone-wrong.

In the 2nd grade musical, I played the role of an incisor;
the entire stage was a mouth,
each tooth a member of the chorus,
the audience seated beneath the opera house chandelier
of the uvula.
A melodrama of dental propaganda,
spotlighting the moral depravity of cavities run amok,
here personified by little imps in black leotards;
of course the toothbrushes had all the good solos.

The director placed me in the back of the risers
like an inept outfielder.
For my costume, I wore the white sheet of a trick-or-treat ghost,
a nondescript tooth joining in the drone of the chorus.

Typecast forever as an incisor,
I found my theatrical motivation and calling:
to become the poet-as-incisor,
to plunge in first
like a little soldier behind the Great War trenches
of wet red lips,
ready to shine in the sudden vulnerability of a smile,
or to deploy in an amphibious landing
known as "bobbing for apples."

I just found out that Neanderthals wore their incisors down to
    the nubs.
The theory: the front teeth held the bear pelt while they skinned
    their kill with a hand axe.
Someday they will mistake poet skulls for Neanderthals.

As a poet, I am armed with the dentist's lamp:
a lighthouse beam with an elbow,

which guides me down down like a shipwreck
into the jagged reef of your smile.

As your poet/dentist here tonight, I
hover like Bela Lugosi with an open cape,
probe the deep pockets of your cheeks with my latex gloves,
silence you with the thick gauze of my stanzas,
and as I begin to drill,
you notice the manicured hedges of my nostrils
and the minty-fresh mysteries contained in my breath
that blows persistently
into your unsuspecting face.

I'M CRAIG THE PLUMBER'S
INCOMPETENT HELPER

the emergency Friday call takes us
way past the Budweiser factory after dark
into the subfreezing Colorado plain
almost out to Wyoming for christssake
to fix the frozen toilet

inside the perimeter fence of the
weird white trash trailer compound

the dwarf in the Burger King Uniform
greets us at the door

and the old man yells at the retarded girl
to tend Cerberus

the plumber leaves me
with the frozen toilet
my job is to tap on the porcelain bowl
so Craig can find the frozen pipes
as he worms across
the length of the crawlspace
darkness beneath

I'm tapping on the porcelain
the retarded girl across the hall kneels
by the door

that separates me the intruder
from the jaws of Cerberus
growling barking clawing the door
and the retarded girl whispers
quiet quiet quiet
in time with the tapping on the porcelain

and I see hanging above the toilet
wooden cross
with a twisted crown-of-thorns
Jesus head in the center disembodied
just the head at the apex
face carved
with the gnarled contortions
of agony
quiet quiet quiet

Craig calls from beneath the trailer
but I can't hear his muffled commands
above the snarling
as Cerberus fantasizes
mauling me
tearing out my throat
the intruder
doesn't matter who
and the relentless
quiet quiet quiet

the dwarf in the Burger King uniform
doesn't help at all
with her employee-discount Whopper by the television

Craig surfaces again

after inhaling the fiberglass insulation beneath
it turns out the pipes are PVC after all so
he can't melt the ice with the blow torch
anyway it was all for nothing
the old man doesn't thank us

and Craig drives us away
as he coughs fiberglass
and the retarded girl appears in our headlights
at the perimeter fence
and do her crossed eyes meet mine I can't tell
for a minute I think she's a clone
how did she get to the gate so fast

and she closes the gate behind us
sealing their otherness
away from me thankchrist and I admire
my James Dean face in the mirror
against the backdrop of the frozen nothingness
and I yearn to scrub
with soap and water
my perfect
incompetent hands

MY QUEER HORROR

I decide to kill my horror novel:
pound the stake into its heart,
fills its lung with sand,
drag it hissing into the sunlight
where it disintegrates into an ashy pile
of all the cigarette butts
I smoked while writing it.

I collected old radio shows
released on cassette
like the story of the young straight couple
moving into the old house with
the locked closet door
no one possesses the key to open. When the blood starts
seeping into the carpet from
underneath the door,
and the moaning emerges

I turned off the cassette player.

I grew up with monsters in my brain.
My earliest nightmare:

The back yard on Winchester street.
A cyclone bursts from the sand box,
scatters plastic pail and shovel.
The witch rises from the sand

with her warlock at her side,
dressed in potato sack rags and stolen shrouds,
hair like corpses drowned on the beach:
my new parents from below
come to claim me
and drag me into their muddy hell.

All the horror stories
crawled with Satan semen
to fertilize my brain.

After reading the first page of the horror novel,
I banished it beneath the bed;
it described the Satanic pentagram, which branded the image
forever on my frontal lobe
where it throbbed like a beacon for Satan
to come collect me.

The Calvin Cadets, my church boy scout group, all stand
in prayer formation
in my basement bedroom:
pledge of allegiance to Jesus,
waiting for the meeting to begin with a salute,
but we lost our American Flag, and
I discover my basement bedroom stretches into the distance
of the underworld
with swampy mud floor. One of the cadets
spots the zombie corpse rising from the mire.
We must call the police someone says, but before they arrive,
the quicksand swallows the corpse back into the depth,
and it waits for me like an unrequited love.

And the dream when I stand with the Calvin Cadets on Golgotha:

Satan hides inside a Calvin Cadet disguise,
but we don't know which boy, so we play
a duck-duck-goose game. When someone says
goose on Satan's head, the boy implodes
as if the body-shell contained nothing but pressure,
hollow like a doll head—a flesh basketball.

I started reading Dracula,
but I stopped in panic when Mina
slurps blood from the open vein on Dracula's bare chest.

Satan drove a purple Camaro
with leather seats:
he pulled up next to me as I walked home from school.
Satan sweated on the leather,
wore shiny purple lipstick and nail polish.
I could see the large pointed nipples on his chest,
which he offered for me
to suck.

ZOMBIE HORDE

It's Xmas Eve and
the zombie horde gathers
like every Tuesday
for brains in my back yard
and they leave the gate unlatched again
for my dog to run away

and Bloody Mary comes through the portal
of the bathroom mirror without any eponymous chanting
and I give her a sponge bath in the tub
and we discuss the brainwash vanities of the
cosmetics industry

and my plumbing shop
sponsored the zombie horde again this year
like a little league team
with adjustable snap ball caps and
fiery-sleeved jerseys

and all of my certified callused plumbers write poetry
unplug horrifying obstructions
like Mary's bandages and cigarette butts
and numerous varieties of rejected pets
that form colonies in the sewers

so merry Xmas sings the zombie horde
and it's just another day closer to nuclear holocaust

and my bomb shelter now holds enough DVDs to reach
my 70th birthday
and I smashed all the bathroom mirrors
down below
and if my dog comes home I'll
never hear the scratching through the concrete
so its merry Xmas at the end of the world
and if I grow old I will never see

UNDERTOW

The search for theme
    ends
and the map dissolves in rain

I need no parachute here:
    the descent not gravity
    but to succumb
    on the flytrap tongue

of the undertow

Innocence:
the swollen eyes of newborn blind

A pink mouse wriggles
    a pink mouse thrown from the nest to burn in the fire of the
    sun

Setting:
The field behind the house where the narrator smokes and the
    blank tapestry of the landscape reflects back the inside of his
    skull

To name the field a stage
reduces the setting to a plane
    where the visible occurs
    where the audience perceives motivation

where action is the storyteller
but this field is a stage in darkness
where the audience worms through
     death-mud darkness

The death of the queer mentor:

When they store your breath away
when you fold inanimate
I will march you down the aisle
twelve legs circle you like a SWAT team
like a wolf pack
like vulture revolution

twelve legs deliver
    one mind
       to the void

The impact of diagnosis punctured

His chest X-ray fled the screen (laugh track)
leaving the black spots behind
to devour him

The narrator's head is a lampshade over a shattered bulb

The flowers scream at him from the median

The narrator never understood the undertow

The narrator never understood the labyrinth of veins
never understood obstructions

The undertow pulls him through the queer hole
   where he chokes on his shadow

The narrator throws his brain in the river
and kneels on the shore where
the forest deer lap dew
   from the hole in his skull
   forever afterward
   amen

THE RAPIDS AND THE RAFT

On the highway,
the drowning of man in the
   riptide of the blind spot.

I lost myself
   to the still black river
man brings his motion to.

Concrete Bleeds with a voice.

The Skin of America,
   shed and abandoned
   grafted by the men
   who tame the bulldozers
   and leave orange cones like buoys.

The road, the unraveled labyrinth,
promises deliverance and rebirth,
   then wraps around your throat
   like an umbilical cord.

The motion of vehicles on the road form
   waves
   currents
   undertows.

The asphalt steals fury from the sun.

The road,
      the circulation of the machine,
      the lanes bovine gateways,
      the swollen abdomen, the industry.

Mail order your rubber monkey.

The sunshine.
There is an absence in the sunshine today.
It seeks me under the pillows.
There is no God in the sunshine today.
The heat erases my mind and drops coal in my hate.
There is an absence of God in the sunshine today.

BABEL

Field notes inside the shark cage:

The traffic on the highway generates
a churning of the unseen
in the roadside bar
like currents through portholes
in a cruise ship on the floor of the abyss
a dock as far below understanding
as a tower reaches above
         to know

The sun in this depth of smoke and volume
is the molten movement beneath
leaking heat through ruptured floor
fractured hull
the influence of constellations
is replaced by the destiny of magma
        we burrow for

The neon bulbs
nesting on ledges in the bar
read the secret of luminescence
the flickering language of the deep
the babble of the void
where volume drowns the lung
and confounded language becomes the code of
    the fixed fish eye

Miles of pressure
history like a vise
deforms the dwellers of crevices
they dislodge from the bar
to float into the dance floor
                    statues into lava

The churning leads to eruption
not the first blast of an island mountain
whose top may reach unto heaven
but the scattering
        upon the face of the earth

HOW I FAILED TO QUIT SMOKING

The anchors of lung cancer:

The narrator's lungs
    a pond
where tadpoles branch legs in bronchial tubes
and mutate in dead ends of the labyrinth
      ecosystem of The Cancer Wheel

Twist my identity around the cigarette
Drop coins to start The Cancer Wheel

The dead are angry at this delay
    The dead deserve improved service

The dead desire company
    The afterlife just another nursing home

Inside the coffee ring where the Lord's face appeared
Inside The Cancer Wheel
    a cycle of precipitation and evaporation
    of huffing and puffing

Hemoptysis
    step right up

INDOCTRINATION

The ultimate job hunting guide:

I feel the Jesus filter me.
Join us.
Digits need the palm.
Your desk next to mine and mine together.
We file your refuse for evaluation.
The uniform is you.
Your penis is our pleasure.
A saddle for your station.
A steed that knows our mind.
We measure your amazement, and trim your excess.

I think this position sounds like an exciting opportunity with
    varied and challenging tasks. It is clear that your company
    offers vital and fascinating technology.

One hundred warm palms to welcome you.
Digits need the palm as drones the queen.
Many cameras in the world today
for the brain collecting.
Let our branches shade your conscience
from the burns of solitude.

To demonstrate my skills in a rewarding career while
    participating in a vital cause.

The uniform is you.
Tie rooted to the heart.

To demonstrate my skills as a team player while participating in
the advancement of a vital cause.

We request your membership.
Your absence pains our extremities.
You are the digit we need for the hand.
Your loyalty embraces our roots.
The entanglement is not strangulation.
To demonstrate my skills as a team player while growing in
experience and product knowledge.

The beak is at the bottom of the octopus embrace.

THE AMERICAN DREAM

the vermin penetrate the house
bring the entire family to the lynching
the ovipositor is full
ride the wheel
    eat a meal

fertilize a tear from a schoolboy
    with the semen of an old man
plant the seed
    a tree will grow

      for all the neighborhood children to hang themselves on

BAR SONGS

there is a ghost in the bar

it watches from the shadows of Happy Hour

standing behind the bar
at first a shark cage from the fondlers in the dark
later to become a stage
sometimes they sing to me
songs of barracudas to guppies
    stares
    dollar bills
    conversations
axes to extract me from the cage
of my own paranoia
    internalized homophobia (the mirror)

the owner of the bar tells me he plans to extract his teeth
then honey I could give you a thrill he says
    gums of fellatio
    god's secret orifice
    mastication of desire

the polar bear stalks holes in the ice where seals emerge for
    oxygen
    the gum hole lurks above the zippers of boys
similar to the adaptation of the constrictor
the jaw dislodges to swallow hole

my dignity becomes the legs of a grasshopper
sticking out the lips of a frog

THE BARTENDER'S MAGIC SHOW

I hoped the bar to be a stage
for the ballet of liquor
the hiss of the soda gun
like distant applause
the pirouette of straws
and the percussion of ice cubes
but my choreography became a magic show
wringing rum from dollar bills
banishing glares of seclusion around the bar
with smoke and secret words

Watch me transform a vessel of glass
to a message of felicity
your belly an ear canal for the whisper of pours
and this miraculous liquid
will sing to your bloodstream
like a letter of requited love

A volunteer from the audience please

Watch
as I pull a chilled shot from behind your ear
the audience can see your head is an empty box

Bottoms up
return it to your head by way of stomach
through the mystery of sleight of hand

ladies and gentleman
it appears again before you in a tumbler
a trick of ritual repetition
the shot mixes with the magic word deep in the brain
and the icy concoction becomes a candle flame
in the concrete wax of your mind
melts down behind your nose
lights up and softens your eyes
loosens the strait jacket buckles of the tongue
the wax careens through your limbs
a signal of ecstasy down the nervous system
frees the hands to touch tight denim
lubricates the knees
and you become an eddy of lava
through the arctic of the dance floor

The conclusion of this magic trick
occurs in the night after last call
if you're lucky
clap your hands
believe in magic
you'll see my miraculous wax
drain out in a splash
against the abdomen of a stranger

After the finale and curtain call
when my sleeves are empty
except for pigeon dung and dollar bills
I see the anonymous fingers of the customers
peeking out beneath the red asbestos curtain
looking for more
I could hold these wandering digits
between my fingers and in my palm

caress the wrinkles of knuckles
trace inflated veins with my thumb
draw the forearms from the curtain
like roots of trees from soil
or I could pluck the bills from their hands
and stamp the fingers away
like rattlesnake hatchlings

RUBBER MONKEYS

A child lost his monkey in the park.
The touch of my finger awakens the demon inside.

It trembles.
It is a sweaty little rubber monkey.

It dances. It is annoying.

I tear the rubber monkey in half.
Now two rubber monkeys dance.

They infuriate me.

The more I tear, the more rubber monkeys.
I do not want to dance with the rubber monkeys.

They divide like cells, breeding with Vermin Speed.
They grow larger,
or I shrink
as the dancing circle of the rubber monkeys includes me,
the welcome of the undertow.
Dance the mad steps with a smile.
Arms around shoulders.
Unison to perfection.
Arms entwine.
A wheel spinning to the Maelstrom Depth.

I am happy.

PERFORMANCE POEM

In this magical act, I replaced
all the doves with
strange words like
many breeds of different
bat pups
nursing and clutching
the coat of their mother.
Before they flew away on cue
they filled my sleeves with their droppings
and their puddles of urine.
At home I give them hamster wheels,
but here in this auditorium,
they focus their aggression on me.

Many words from previous rehearsals for this poem
flew up into the corners and crevices of the ceiling
where they mated
and multiplied,
and their droppings fall down on your heads
like drops of urine from the ceiling
in a gigantic roosting cave.
They elected a leader, a hive queen
that will fly down and perch on my arm
like a ventriloquist's dummy
or a nursing baby
or an evil homunculus
to feed and get more wet language.

If you look up,
one of the weird ideas floating around this room
might land on your eyeball,
burrow into your brain,
and you would never be the same again.
Some of my language might swim away to follow
larger poems like
remoras following a great white shark.

My language is wet
because the mammalian brain package
is wet.
I read like a dog licks skin
to absorb it into my wet package,
calm and complete inside my body.

The language swims and intersects
in there,
in the warm wet mammalian package.

For my next magical trick,
my shadows might dance upon the wall
and never leave.
Or, I might desperately
turn to the lost art of juggling
butcher knives,
or sticking my arm outside the shark cage.

This might take a long time
This might end the war.

Prayers are words perhaps and never

marginal
often composed of words perhaps.
When you're in trouble, I guess you
know it.

SCHOOL ZONE

He likes to be the crossing guard,
rolling cigarettes with extra squares of gauze
while waiting for the bell at the intersection,
shaving with the edge of the STOP sign paddle
designed for First Aid amputations.
Escorting the wheelchairs to safety,
he shines the smile of a merry convict
concealing a cafeteria spoon,
huffing just enough to fill small lungs.

He kisses the mothers' babies, of course,
embarrassed when his tongue catches
on the scalps of the unbaptized,
frozen flagpoles of skull.
Like an ethereal ear of a fetal pig,
his tongue floats after the children
to groom all the sidewalk roses in their path.
His sunshine never terrifies
when glaring off the windshield
of his approaching angel,
and all his zippers extend to the head.

WARNING

Like something dismembered
sailing through the mail
to horrify the estranged,
a meteor as large as an ark
slides into the atmosphere
with the destiny of an earthworm on sidewalk,
possessing a subtle radiation
that can at last return arms to the serpent.

The rock is now the size of a bomb shelter
that molds under the tender epidermis of Earth.
Like a strain that still withers in the mosquito's needle,
it must forsake impact
as the stratosphere burns it down to the dimensions
of a hot coffin for a breathless horseman.

A prophetic dream that can't follow
through the layers of waking,
the streak of light evokes the fascination of the rainbow,
but it lacks the covenant,
a bottle against an impenetrable hull.

THE RINGMASTER

won't negotiate.
He crashes in with the Virus Skill
to plant the fever that murmurs truth
behind the lies of a microphone.

When scandal blooms,
it incites the internal frenzy
of a guillotine in a psycho ward,
a busy little hive forever afterwards.

THEN MY BRAIN CHANGED IN THE SPACE OF A GASP

as I stepped back into the periphery of watchers.
My sutures parted in the inhalation
like the crumbling chest of a statue
inspired to scream,
and little humps of brain jutted out the gaps
like too many rodent muzzles
pressing through bars in curiosity or desperation.
Knowing filled my mind as if eyeballs were nostrils
whiffing dark truth.

All the gray tubes in my head,
once round like the joints of a baby
and soft as the cheeks of the drowned,
now stretched out to sprint,
flexing like muscles in leotards on a stage.

Each morning I pass the intersection
where the jumper hit sidewalk.
I see the spectral monument that sprouted there,
and the street reeks of a resurrection
or a metamorphosis,
as if the mouse could change into the aerial bat
by watching its brother ascend on black wings.

THE ENEMY EVOLVES

Circuitry melts into veins.
The trees bear photosynthetic eyes
that absorb my movements,
and my October lawn becomes their cutting room floor.

They engineer clones who wear pearls
and never orgasm.
I married one.
Her poisons smell like dust,
activating if I resist suggestion.
The pregnancies were convincing.
Now I'm outnumbered in my own home.
The children stand motionless
like specimens in jars of formaldehyde
until I turn the doorknob
and catch them in mid-motion.
Directives line up in every hallway of their flesh
like chromosomes.

They replaced my dog with a replica
that lapped milk in Morse code.
I detected humming from the cranium,
and its blood shined with rainbows
of liquid programming.
Of course it's dangerous to execute spies
because their blood is distinctly radioactive.
Only the color can be washed away.

My name is written on the Master Assassin's abdomen,
coded in kinky black hairs.
He commissions artificial spiders
whose webs catch my vibrations
and store intelligence in silky egg sacs.
He only answers to the brain in the pumpkin shell
they grow beneath the doll factory.
The agents process information into adrenalin
to inject into the pumpkin,
and the organ becomes a god.

I GLIMPSED IT THROUGH THE FIRE

where the distortion of heat painted its clarity.

To reproduce the final symmetry,
this boundary to The Void,
I might turn X-ray machines
on the brain of a dead genius.

The spider's web is a simple hole
compared to its complexity,
and what we might catch in its articulation
could unite severed spinal cords,
strike a fatal hole
in the skull of The Virus,
and return the blasted shrapnel
to within the shell of war.

But the sign is a tattoo on an infant's chest
that grows beyond our understanding.

If only the ants in their limitless horde
could form its constellation,
or the maggots build a voice box
to sound the pitch of the sign,
but the sign bounces like the scream of the bat
and would only escape in the echo.

For the sign is not only in the design of the silk veil,
but in the enactment of the dance
between spinneret and the orifice,
the cocoon and its enumeration.

Human fingernails grow after death,
but never long enough to scratch the depth of its message
on the inside of a pine box.

Because the sign is the network,
the burrow of the worm,
the sign in the meal of my mind,
spoken on the frequency
of the cold bone.

REFRAIN

I glimpsed the sign in fire
where heat distortion clarified
the symmetry,
a web to snare an articulation
to unite the severed spinal cords.

The final sign,
a silk veil composed
by spinneret and orifice.

The network,
the burrow of the worm
in my mind,
a cocoon growing
enumeration
on the frequency
of the cold bone.

THE MOON DRIPS BLOOD ON FLIGHTLESS DOVES

Monstrous goats buck the wicked.
Rigor Mortis turns a mother's lap to stone,
and her babe rolls off to dust.
Supernatural perversions burst from Hell
like children from a schoolhouse,
an aerial parade of fangs and serpent wings
while stars fall like brilliant figs.

What an unpleasant mess of turbulent clouds,
crushed horses, and dangling corpse bosoms.
This apocalypse is ridiculous.
The undertaker Darkenbrook was right about Revelations,
but I fancied the figurative.
I will wait until this literal foolishness
passes back to print,
if I can withstand the odor of subterranean breath.

I once believed prayer scriveners
who lounged on rosy buttocks in beds of clouds
recorded every syllable of my prayers;
fulfillment of prophecy
forces me to pray to them again
to beg for complexity.
Open the seals with ceremony.
Darkenbrook taught me that dignity
should always dress death.

Here he comes on that pale horse.
Feeling cross and frightful?
Looks like Grandfather after the dawn milking.
Plucked from the pyre at the last minute?
What a tarnished thing he wears,
not a proper crown.
I'd expect excellent forging from his country.

I've read Revelations often.
I hoped for a fine, noble King of Death.
Grim, of course, ravishing,
but in shadowy robes of grace.
More like Darkenbrook in tails.
His horse should be a handsome thing,
pale like marble, not lacking hue.

I wonder if Death keeps a lady,
and if she approves of him trampling enraptured virgins
and never bathing.
She must wear an exquisite burial gown
like the widow who fell beneath her horse.
The angelic fabric floated above her mangled frame
in the coffin, concealing injuries
like a bed of fog with frosty lace.

Poor Darkenbrook.
He falters on the ground before me.
Do you not see me in my hiding place?
Has this apocalypse consumed you too?
Remember the delightful jokes about the locust
with the lady's hairstyle?

Perhaps my figurative readings can comfort you.

I think I did welcome your attention.

Sister said she feared death to know
you would dress her,
but I never did.

GOODBYE CIRCULATION

So I said Goodbye to Circulation
and the Blue-Ball Circumambulation
of every goddamn thing I ever cared about,
of every goddamn thing.

So Goodbye Circulation,
and I can only hope for good this time,
and I can only hope for good.
Goodbye Hamster Wheel Interstate.
Goodbye inviolate Blue Egg Nightmare
in the Robin's Nest of cash and bones.

Time to reorder
a new shipment of body bags for the inmates
at Mount Salvation psychiatric facility
for the meat inside the shell
of strait jackets
in this America my sausage factory,
here in the witch-hunting cacophony.

Time to worship more than white mountain faces,
false minted icon idols.
Time to dehumanize the poodles
and the White Christian Fetus,
not the car bomb babies
in black plastic gurney descents.

Every camera in America flattens;
American voices
streams of words
to fill our Hindenburg Balloons of patriotism,
all our iron hulls
banging iceberg percussion.

So Goodbye Circulation,
and the Blue-Ball Circumambulation
of every goddamn thing I ever cared about,
of every goddamn thing.

Sweet Dreams
Sweet Flatline
Sweet Sausage Factory Convolutions
and Sodium Pentathol declarations of love.

Just like you said:
meaningless shit pervades the landscape,
and Circulation can run without me.

Goodbye Circulation
Goodbye Hamster Wheel,
and I know it's all Meaningless Shit,
but Circulation can run without me.

SUMMERTIME

I loved you in the summertime
when the rain carried the bodies
of the fallen birds away,
when the dust arose from the bedroom floor
to float in the beam of sunlight,
when the match burnt out
before reaching your finger,
when the Queen Bee chose your eaves
to create her hundred million,
when our shadows merged
on the wall of the tent.

I loved you in the summertime
before they drained the pools,
before the vessels broke,
before the mosquito thirst,
before the sun dropped deep in its grave.

PUBLIC SERVICE ANNOUNCEMENT

The Fade In is not the flash of eyelids
or the stagger of curtains on a rod.
The Fade In is that sudden light
when captors open a trunk
or a burial plays in reverse,
not the tunnel of headlights approaching,
but the blur and focus of breaking a plane of water
and the vacuum of lost breath
only to parch in this setting:

A scene of desolation:
A four-lane highway in a setting to be recognized as Wyoming.
Wind.

The Camera,
that filter of lenses like spectacles of a stranger,
the eavesdropper who steps over wires to the stage,
whose mind is not the soft, warm
package of the mammal,
but a network of metal,
frames the scene like a windshield filthy
with dust and nicotine.

Of course, the soundtrack plays here.
Similar to a shell at the ear,
the score moves in microcosm,
a fly that crept up the canal to the drum.

It knew the eyeballs of raccoons as a maggot on the roadside,
knew wind beyond endurance of mammalian squinting.
The fly knows the road,
forsakes a tradition of buzzing
for a communication of truth.
Safe at last from the tyranny of wind,
it sings in the ear of the audience
and plays the trick of the shell.

Focus on the wreckage.
One less body bag in the ambulance.
One body bag closer to a new package of body bags
like a box of tissues. Pull out one,
up pops the next.
The fly sings a song of zippers.

The body bags are kept on the top shelf in the ambulance,
     more out of superstition than convenience, next to a spiral
     notebook with "Victim's Last Words" written on the cover in
     permanent marker.

The Notebook Entry:
Help.
My leg.
I have blood.
The wind. The wind.

Close up on
the survivor,
the boy with the earring that dangles.
This earring, now weathered by wind on the roadside,
followed the metamorphosis of wind chimes
from charming to terrifying in the escalation of storms.

Deep in the bomb shelter of his mind,
he flinches at the clangor.

The camera crew left for home after filming a segment for the
    latest installment in a series of public service announcements
    and driver's education instructional videos that feature a
    ruddy Hollywood favorite and The Hall of Bloody Prom
    Dresses, a museum of Prom Night death, a monument to
    iniquity and drunk driving.

Close up on
the studio janitorial staff sweeping bits of beer bottle and
    windshield beneath the hems.

Falling leaves.

Our spokesman, known for a span of fame portraying police
    officers characterized by quick excesses of violence, resists
    the similarity between the row of pretty dresses and the
    mystery of his mother's bedroom closet.

For a meager restitution to the survivor,
the studio assigns a purpose to the car accident
like a campfire story
or a threat.
The survivor prefers the footage
that wanders across his sight in television commercials
and cauterizes
unlike the flow of his memory.

After they removed his boyfriend in a body bag,
the survivor speaks his lines:
It is August,

the month of highway death,
and the sunshine lost god.
All vehicles of motion have reefs to wreck upon.
The road is no longer a plane.
Potholes are cracks in the ice.
Asphalt remains impenetrable,
but no longer stagnant.
The car may travel parallel through infinity,
but I am forever perpendicular
and planted.
The cameras crash into my brain
and perform a puppet show on my face.

Our spokesman buckles his seat belt in honor of the dead
and the fly sings of crevices.

MY HEAD IS A CATHEDRAL

I capture the voices
like fireflies
in mason jars

some boil with rage
and evaporate
through the holes
in the lid

others percolate
the past
and the jar is filled
with darkness

the most frightening voices
spin cocoons
but I place those jars
in the freezer

at last
free of the voices
my mind is placid
like a windexed mirror

and I see in the reflection
my head is a cathedral
from which the gargoyles have flown

SHADOW

My Shadow is here;
it likes to remind me
of missed turns, lost maps,
and every single compass that
I dropped off a cliff.

I try
to erase it
like whitening toothpaste,
and it stays with me,
whispering comments
from bad report cards.

I can't drown it in the fish tank,
or wash it away in the laundry machine,
or catch it in the strait jacket mousetrap.

I try
to eradicate it
like bleach on grass stains;

I try
to rip it out by the seams,

and it returns.

My Shadow is here;
it likes to remind me
of my telescopes in the cellar,
swallowed contact lenses,
and foggy binoculars,

but pills don't lessen it;
the doctor can't chop it,
and when I yell at it with
my best impression of
a lion tamer,
I just get a sore throat,

and then I remember:
despair is a life raft on lava,

and in the end,
I bring my shadow to bed with me,
wrap it around me like a
delicate cocoon membrane.

And now I take My Shadow
with me to visit the zoo
where we feel sorry together
for majestic and powerful
creatures
behind glass cages
like I used to be.

THE PHOENIX KIT

Finally sick of shopping for miracles,
I find the phoenix kit in aisle 7,
next to the lighter fluid,
charcoal briquettes,
and campfire logs in the
ready-to-burn bags.
Packaged in a little cardboard box
like a TV dinner
with dual directions
for fireplace or microwave oven,
the phoenix kit finds its way
into my shopping cart.

I lift the proper flaps to transform
box packaging to phoenix birth-pyre,
and cut open the freshness pouch
to remove my bird-effigy:
a little bundle of sticks, tissue paper,
and cinnamon twigs tied to resemble
the majestic harbinger from the world of myth.

I prop it up on the pyre, set the bic lighter
to the tabs labeled "burn here,"
touch the flame to my cigarette,
and wait.

First it burns out, of course,

then it rises up again
like a cross between a puppet
and a sparkler,
flying up the chimney, and out
into the sky.
I run outside to see it dissipate
like just another firecracker.

Next I ignore the old directions on the box,
remove the dead fetus
from the cage in my chest,
naked and limp in my hand
like a salmon,
and I burn it on the nest of my
wadded-up journal entries.

I feel the second-guess spark of panic,
but then the phoenix rises again,
this time
posing like an overdramatic crest,
the arrogance of the eagle.

With the resonant voice of an Old-Testament bush,
the majestic phoenix speaks my name.
I name him Clarence,
give him a litter box in the laundry room
where I wait with my plastic clawed pooper-scooper.

It turns out that every charcoal black phoenix turd
is a fortune cookie.
Again and again I dig out the fortune.
Always the same, it reads:
Assembled in China.

HELLO FEAR

You,
the one always clutching the bullhorn
as if
I might fight you for it.

You should seek work
narrating the trailers
for cheezy Satan movies. You,
always the break-in voice of
the Emergency Broadcast System,
freaking me out with
crescendo warnings of the imminent
Flash Flood
and the pinwheel touchdown of the
Mega-Twister, all perpetual haunters
of the View-Master in my mind.

My brain becomes your radio too
sometimes
for the latest broadcast of
the Orson Welles Panic Hour,
firing up my amygdala,
the almond-shaped fear nugget that
operates roller coasters in my mind,
the ones packed with an
all-star cast of screamers.

Hey listen, Fear, my nemesis, my baby,
you, the tremulous force field like an
ice-cold amniotic sac, always
surrounding me,
drowning me,
why not take a Hawaiian vacation
for once,
or hibernate yourself away
down deep in the silent archive of
squirrel acorns—out of my head and
just where I can find you.

THE FEAR IN MY HEART

Before I read your book,
I tried to remove the obstruction
of my fear like
wriggling out
slippery meat from
cracked crab legs
or sucking out
rattlesnake poison from
shins.

I tried to be polite like
asking fire to hold its tongue
or the undertow to release
its noose,
but the fear only gripped me
like talons in the skin of a rabbit,
and I was a cricket
in the cage of a fist.

After I read your book,
I unwrapped the fear
like mummy gauze from clear blue eyes,
like strait jackets
from acrobats.

And then I chose to live in every nook and
cranny between

moments
where the tick of a clock opens
down the alleyways of the atom.
Here my fingers pulled the plug,
and my fear followed the spiral descent,
a bathtub release
down the gurgle of a drain.

SOMETIMES MY WORDS ARE TIMID BUMBLEBEES

They never intend to sting,
only to pollinate.
They founder in the entanglement of spider lines
erected between our pillows.
They drown in the pouring of concrete foundations
for another useless battlement.

The same tongue that launches
these ill-fated and misunderstood drones
communicates a wet, wordless truth,
enters and flickers in the warm center of your anus.
My words attempt to echo this tender truth,
but the melodious hum of bumblebee unison is scattered
and battered into babble
by conflict.
The abandoned hive embodies
the desiccation of understanding.

Every time you penetrate me,
it is the peck of freedom for the hatchling to emerge
from the suffocating leather of egg skin.

Every time you penetrate me,
it is the opening of the molting hole,
to shed the old dead skin of my past
that I drape over coat hangers

next to old mummies.

Each ejaculation inside me
is a warm eddy
to resurrect a hypothermic heart.

Sometimes my words are timid bumblebees,
but each carries pollen
in the dense hair of minute appendages.
Together we can clear away
the concrete.
Sometimes my words are timid bumblebees,
but each carries the seed,
a note in the chord,
a character in the text.

A RECIPE FOR SPONTANEOUS HUMAN COMBUSTION

Pour buckets of chum off a life raft and wait
for the vibrating kernels of hate in your mind.
Epinephrine ignites when you make yourself bait.

Search for gorgeous car accidents and participate
in hopeless CPR on the victims you find.
Pour buckets of chum off a life raft and wait.

Attend a cardboard church with your murderous hate.
Find a shepherd boy and spank his behind.
Epinephrine ignites when you make yourself bait.

Dissect a swamp frog on an offering plate.
Place the swallowed fireflies between your teeth and grind.
Pour buckets of chum off a life raft and wait.

Sprint in black corduroy while you ruminate.
Hide match heads in the cigarettes of the blind.
Epinephrine ignites when you make yourself bait.

Shout blasphemy under lightning and never hesitate
to leave love and suicide notes unsigned.
Pour buckets of chum off a life raft and wait.
Epinephrine ignites when you make yourself bait.

THE DAY WE MET

We both escaped the body bag on the day we met
when we giggled about fractured orbital sockets
after the Great Ferris Wheel Disaster.
You kissed away my minor head injury,
and when I gave you my phone number
on a strip of gauze,
a wisp of cotton candy still clung to your hair.

After the day we met,
I found the courage
to put down the suffering dog of my childhood
and no longer heard the mournful cries of hip dysplasia
and lost walks in the park.
The generations of rodents beneath the floorboards
at last shared the dosages of cyanide
I left for them every Sunday beneath the sink.
The evil spirit that haunted the bedroom,
after years of coaxing,
politely asked for directions out the window.
I cut down all my nooses tied to rafters in the garage,
motivated the agoraphobic bee hive
to scour the back yard for eager stamens,
and discovered all the eyes of my paranoia
to be finally fixed and dilated.

Your light reaches into the skull I wear;
your smile killed all my warts.

I would gladly swing the ax for you,
brave dismemberment on the assembly line
for you.
From this day, I pledge
to share all your carcinogens forever.

Lightning Source UK Ltd.
Milton Keynes UK
UKHW041014050420
361341UK00001B/33